treasure the
m o ments

Spiritual Insights for Motherhood

Laurel Hildebrandt

TATE PUBLISHING, LLC

Scripture quotations marked "NIV" are taken from the Holy Bible, New
International Version ®, Copyright © 1973, 1978, 1984 by International
Bible Society. Used by permission of Zondervan Publishing House. All rights
reserved.

Scripture quotations marked "NKJV" are taken from The New King James
Version / Thomas Nelson Publishers, Nashville: Thomas Nelson Publishers.
Copyright © 1982. Used by permission. All rights reserved.
Barber, Katherine, The Canadian Oxford Dictionary Oxford University
Press Canada, Oxford, Ont. 1998
Brother Lawrence The Practice of the Presence of God Whitaker House,
United States. 1982

This book is designed to provide accurate and authoritative information
with regard to the subject matter covered. This information is given with the
understanding that neither the author nor Tate Publishing, LLC is engaged
in rendering legal, professional advice. Since the details of your situation
are fact dependent, you should additionally seek the services of a competent
professional.

ISBN: 1-9332904-2-0

I Dedicate this book . . .

. . . as a labor of love to my two children, Donovan and Joshua, who are helping me learn to be a godly Mom.

. . . to my husband, Glen, who travels with me in this strange and marvelous journey.

Acknowledgments

~Primarily, I thank God for giving me insight and wisdom thus far in the world of being a mom, helping me write this book, and blessing me with a wonderful husband and children.

~I would also like to thank April Yamasaki for proofreading the first draft and giving me suggestions and encouragement throughout the writing and publishing process.

~I thank my husband, Glen, for allowing me to sit at the computer and write and for being the godly man of integrity that he is.

~I want to thank Donovan and Joshua for being my children and inspiring this book.

~I give thanks to the many friends who would read a chapter and encourage me to keep going.

~I also would like to thank the many people at Tate Publishing for believing in me, encouraging me, being excited with me, and publishing *Treasure the Moments*.

~I would like to thank Helma Sawatzky for her wisdom, sensitivity and expertise in doing a final read for me.

~I give a huge thanks to my mom and dad who helped shape my character into the person I am today. They raised me in a godly home, introduced me to my Lord and Savior, and taught me Christ-like values through word and deed. Their support has been unending, even into adulthood. For this, I am truly grateful.

~Equal thanks are due my mother-in-law and father-in-law for raising Glen to be a godly man and husband, their complete acceptance and love for me from day one, the friendship and parenting they have offered me, and the huge support for this book. They have gifted me in word and deed. Their generosity and their hearts are huge. I see Jesus in them, and I am truly grateful.

Table of Contents

Foreword

I have been privileged to witness *Treasure the Moments* grow from a glimmer of an idea, to a few chapters of text, to the finished manuscript you now hold in your hands. It's at once a uniquely personal book, where you'll enter the home and daily lives of Laurel, Glen, and their two children—Donovan and Joshua. Yet it is also a book filled with universal truth—God's unconditional love and enduring presence in the midst of everyday life.

In these pages, you will find some happy moments that will make you smile, some tender moments that will move you to tears, and through it all, a God who is ever loving and ever faithful. Written in an engaging, personal tone, like one friend talking to another, the short chapters are just right to read in snatches during your own busy day. As you read, may you also reflect on your own home and family life, and learn to treasure the moments of your day.

- April Yamasaki, Author and Pastor

Introduction

Written as "moments" that happened during Joshua's first year, *Treasure the Moments* is a labor of love for my two children, Donovan and Joshua. As I was spending some time writing in my journal I found myself drawing parallels to Mary, the mother of Jesus. I was searching for a spiritual lesson and searching for a way to become a better mom. Educationally, I have a Master's degree in counselling, yet the art of "mothering" presents no diploma. I read the regular amount on parenting and tried to put principles that I agreed with into practice. My prayer each day was (and still is), "Lord, guide my every word as I raise these beautiful children that you have entrusted to me." Learning to be a good mom seemed to depend on me actually doing it—relying on God for wisdom, strength, words, and caring, just as I do in my life in general and as a professional counsellor.

In the midst of the beginnings of this learning to be a mom, I struggled with two years of severe sleep deprivation throughout my last pregnancy and Joshua's first year. I needed to find sanity somewhere. The outlet and sanity came in the writing of *Treasure the Moments.* It was while I was writing that I had my quiet moments of sanity and could clearly hear God's voice. The words flowed as God showed me the spiritual principles and lessons that I could learn as a mother from the most wonderful book on parenting, God's Word, the Bible.

The purpose for writing *Treasure the Moments* soon expanded. A deeper vision took root as I shared my newly learned lessons and newly written chapters with friends. They laughed and cried with me as I read them chapters over the phone. They learned with me and drew closer to God as a result. The purpose for writing was now to reach more mothers and share what God was teaching me. It was, in essence, a normalization of all the strange, humorous, and scary moments of being a mother. It was a normalization of the emotions that shoot through a mother as her hormones stabilize—in a setting of little to no sleep. It became an encouragement to mothers everywhere, whether in a two-parent family or a single-parent family, to keep going, to keep relying on God, to loosen up the perfectionistic standards we set for ourselves, and to do our best as we stay firmly rooted and grounded in God. As I continued to write the purpose also came to include fathers. Without them, a mother's job is more difficult. I wanted to encourage fathers to understand what goes on during any given day within the household and to perhaps learn how their wives think. Part of the goal of writing was also to encourage them to be godly fathers and husbands.

While these purposes were in mind, I wanted to write something that was easily readable in a relatively short amount of time that would bring a smile to the face of the reader—a story whereby a lesson was learned. *Treasure the Moments* became distinctive in that I share real life moments from my own life, in many ways becoming vulnerable to the reader and allowing them into my life and home. From these moments, I draw spiritual life lessons that can be treasured. Within the contents of *Treasure the Moments,* the reader will enter into my life, my home, and meet my family. The reader will be introduced to my musings on life as a mom. The reader will be pointed to God, inspired, and challenged to live a godly life.

It is my sincere hope and prayer that *Treasure the Moments* becomes widely read and known as a book of encouragement and inspiration. May the reader be drawn close to God and truly blessed.

Laurel Hildebrandt

Chapter 1

A Higher Calling

"Well, dear," I said as calmly as I could to my sick husband lying on the couch. "I'm pregnant."

How many days do you dream of the moment when you announce to your husband that you're pregnant? How will you say it? How will he react? What will your life hold now? Will everything be absolutely different than it was before? Will it be better? Will it be worse? What kind of child or children will you have? Should you be excited? Nervous? Or just plain scared? The many thoughts that go through your mind when you actually are pregnant, especially for the first time, are almost incomprehensible. The emotions are flying high one minute with the elation of carrying a baby inside you; the next minute your feelings plummet to the ground with nervousness and perhaps a little fear of the unknown.

At times during my first pregnancy, I was downright scared! I had been through years of schooling. I was a certified clinical counsellor holding a Master's degree, teaching a couple of classes at a Bible college, maintaining a private counselling practice, leading a youth group, and counselling out of three other counselling agencies just to pay the bills. I loved being busy. I loved counselling, teaching, and youth pastoring. I had aspirations of going on to get a doctorate in psychology. Then the pregnant word happened. It was planned, but somehow you don't think it will ever happen. When it's just *planned* and not a reality, it's easy to think that life will always be as it always was—busy! In my opinion, getting a Doctorate degree would have been easier than being a mother. However, being the mother of two wonderful boys is definitely much more fun . . .

My husband, still lying on the couch, repeated my word. "Pregnant." He looked at me with his baby blue, gentle eyes—full of wonder, love, amazement, and fear. "Pregnant," he said again. He coughed from his bad cold and dug his head into his pillow. "Pregnant."

I could not keep the smile from my face. I could not speak. I could barely get my shoes off my feet. Finally, I looked up at him and mustered, "Is that all you can say?"

With a grin from ear to ear, his face beamed! "Pregnant," he repeated. Finally, a new word came out of his mouth, "Wow!"

Still in shock, I went to him. Both of us embraced, holding each other tight, not able to say a word. Finally, breaking apart, we looked at each other's large smiles and repeated together, "Pregnant! Wow!"

Although the pregnancy is nine long, laborious months, there is definitely a reason. It takes three months just to get used to the idea of being pregnant. Those first three months are generally the ones where you are the most sick. I was blessed with sickness the whole nine months with both boys so they are both a labor of my love in a very real sense! By the time the nine months are up, they will actually extend into ten full months. By this time, my husband and I were both very ready to have the baby. You want to meet this unnamed child and discover his or her personality outside the womb. You are excited to see whom this child looks like–although it really doesn't matter! You are excited to find out what gender this child is. You are in a dilemma over what to name the child. You have hunted for diapers, Vaseline, cribs, teddy bears, clothes, spit rags, receiving blankets, bottles, and soothers and have absolutely no clue what you are going to do with any of them! All throughout, you wonder - what kind of a mother will I be? Will I be kind and patient and loving and gracious? Or will I yell over "spilled milk"? Will I function on little sleep? Will my baby sleep? You read the latest books and try to have a plan in action. I followed my sister and her baby around as much as I could.

"What are you doing now, Darlene? How do you bathe a baby? How do you change someone so little? What if the baby doesn't sleep? What are you doing now and why?" I'm quite sure I drove her nuts for awhile.

The day is almost there. You've read the books. You've bought the things that everyone says you'll need for a newborn baby. You even have some things for when they graduate from college. You have your plan. You're ready, and you can't stand even one more minute of pregnancy.

Then it happens. Labor. And more labor. And then some more labor. And then a few drugs, a bit of laughing gas. A pediatrician. A roomful of strangers, although I was seeing double for Donovan's birth because of the Demerol. Finally, the last push and you are officially a parent! No more life as you know it. Yet somehow in the nine months it took to form this child, a bond has been formed, and you really don't care that life will never be the same. In fact, you don't want it to be the same. You see the folly of the running around, and in the time it takes to form and laboriously deliver a baby, you have received a new calling from God. You are called to be a mother.

Glen leaned over me and kissed my sweaty brow. He whispered tenderly in my ear, "Donovan's here. I love you." In that moment, though Donovan was in the hands of the pediatrician because of minor complications, I knew that everything would be all right. I knew that I was called to be Donovan's mother.

With Joshua's birth, twenty-two months later, the doctor announced, "It's a boy! You can breathe normally now, Laurel." As I struggled to stop hyperventilating, I knew way down to my deepest spirit that I was called to be Joshua's mother.

I heard God's voice. I heard His voice in Glen's sweet caress of my forehead through each birth. I heard God's voice through holding my sweet, newborn babes on my breast. I heard God's voice through every cry and wail for Mommy, through every "I love you, Mom," and through every adorable look my boys give me.

I heard God's voice very clearly say to me, "Laurel, I have blessed you with two boys. You are called to be their mother. You are still called to be my warrior—to spread peace and my words wherever you go. You are still called to counsel others, but for now—until the boys don't need you nearly as much—your main priority is to be Donovan and Joshua's mother. This is a higher calling than any other I can give you. This is a part of your blessing."

A higher calling—I never concentrated on or longed for children. I always sought how I could best serve the Lord. When God led me into the counselling field, I found (and still find) it exciting, challenging, and fun when I get to witness God's healing power. Yet there is nothing in the entire world that pulls at my heart as much as my boys. I never imagined going to work and leaving my boys, even for one or two days a week, would be so hard. Though my logical mind knows I need a break to be a better mother, it is hard. I miss them when I am not with them. It is quiet.

I still aspire to get a doctorate, if that is where God leads me. Yet I am convinced that nothing in this world could be more exciting, challenging, frustrating, full of fun, and wonderfully fulfilling than being a mother. Nothing could prepare me for these first years of motherhood, and I'm sure nothing can prepare me for the next years of parenthood. Yet I know that this is my higher calling. I gratefully accept this gift from God. I earnestly seek God's guidance in how best to fulfill this calling. At God's throne, I stand in the gap as an intercessor for my boys and daily ask Him to bless them as He has so abundantly blessed my husband and me. May God's will be done in the lives of Donovan and Joshua, as Glen and I attempt to fulfill our calling as Mom and Dad.

Chapter Two
A Day in the Life of . . .

My friend, Sandy, called at 2:10 pm. saying, "Just wondering if you forgot about me?" My brain began a frantic race backward through time. Morning . . . BIG headache. Took painkillers. Changed two diapers. Gave one bath to an 8-week-old Joshua. Ate breakfast amidst loud crying. Headache *still* BIG. I managed to grab a shower in all the chaos and pain of the morning. Finally, we made it out the door with Joshua for a doctor's appointment, with my 2-year-old son Donovan in tow. Next stop, the chiropractor . . . then home to fix lunch and try to get some food down my throat with loud noises and crying all around me. (It's amazing how noisy two very small boys can be!) After changing both boys' diapers came the traditional walking and rocking of Joshua who is plagued with a very sore tummy, which is actually quite severe colic. Then one of the boys was finally sleeping.

Did I forget about my friend? Definitely. Yes. I forgot. I hired Sandy as a contract counsellor for my private counselling practice; I was to meet her one hour before her first client's appointment. I definitely forgot, and Glen had just left to run errands! Thank you, God, for cell phones! One quick call to Glen and he promised to be home in ten minutes. I changed Joshua's diaper again, while cooing and smiling at my poor, little sweetheart with the sore tummy. He was still crying so I resorted to telling stories. For the moment, the sound of my voice quieted him slightly. My sore eyes took in the sight of dishes and food still on the table. The time was already 3:00 P.M. Suddenly, I remembered my counselling practice again and realized I needed to print out some more forms for Sandy's new client.

Glen walked in the door and announced that he needed a nap. He had just been called in to truck the evening/night shift. I don't get a nap because apparently it's not dangerous for me to be at home with two small children. I provide 24-hour-a-day care for both, minus the time I manage to work and counsel others. I start to question my sanity.

Running through my brain was a myriad of events that seemed to prove my self-diagnosis. Today I found the carob sauce in a drawer for plastic storage containers. It belongs in the fridge. During the night, Joshua woke me up three times, staying awake for two hours each time. This morning, I had a migraine that was simply a continuation of the migraine from days and years gone past; it just seems to vary in intensity. Today is also the day I lost a large sum of money in my counselling practice because of a rock-climbing workshop that did not have enough people registered. The workshop was offered to give my counselling intern some more counselling hours and experience, but as it turned out, my intern had a great day rock climbing by himself, at my expense. I guess I should be feeling generous and kind. Part of me feels glad that at least the money spent was not completely wasted. Unfortunately, the other part of me just feels broke, especially with my husband not working full-time right now.

Glen's job fell through when Joshua was 2 weeks old. Now Glen is "relief" trucking to pay for all the things that keep breaking around here and all my business mistakes, but we're not really making a dent on that large line of credit. On the up side, God blessed us with a line of credit, and we're not going further into it . . . yet. That will happen in the fall when Glen starts a Master's degree in counselling. One more month.

Questioning my sanity at this point seems completely

legitimate. My tired brain runs through the juggling act I seem to be performing. I have a 2-year-old. I have a baby who refuses to sleep and cries much of the time. I have a private counselling practice that I can't keep up with because of my lack of sleep. In two weeks, autumn will be upon us, and I start teaching two counselling courses at the local Bible college again. I can barely stay awake to supervise my intern counsellor and have zero time for any administrative work. My self-analysis seems to ring true in my very tired brain. Diagnosis: crazy Mom.

For instance, last night Glen worked. I thought I would be brave and take Donovan and Joshua for a walk in the park by myself. Other moms seem to manage okay. I never hear other children screaming at the top of their lungs in the park. Every child wants to go to the park, right? The plan was set. Of course, Joshua would ride in the stroller, and Donovan could walk. We made it just fine to the park, despite the constant, inner panic whenever cars drove by.

"Stay beside Mommy, Donovan!"

"Car coming!" Panic.

"Don't fall in the water!" More inner panic.

My reasoning told me it would be hard to save a drowning 2-year-old and keep an eye on an infant at the same time. Outwardly, everything was reasonably calm—until we headed home. Donovan very adamantly decided, as only a 2-year-old can, he was going to ride in the stroller. I pushed the stroller with one arm and carried "Baby Josh," as Donovan calls him, in the other arm—all the way home. Did I mention there was quite a long ways to go? Did I say something about a BIG headache? Lack of sleep? Sore back and neck? Did I say "brave"?

I wonder if Mary, the mother of Jesus, felt brave? Were there times when she felt crazy? She was talked to by an angel and informed of Jesus' miraculous entry onto earth—through her willingness. She risked her upcoming marriage to Joseph, her reputation, and even her very life to follow God's directions for her. She was forced to travel a long distance on a donkey, while obviously very pregnant. Sounds crazy to me. Yet I am quite sure that she was completely sane. All Biblical indications are that she entered into the motherhood of Jesus with complete peace and a joy beyond all comprehension because she understood the honor of bearing the Son of God. Mary understood that she had been called for this purpose in her life and completed trusted God with her calling, no matter what the consequences.

There is a fine line between brave and crazy. I know that I feel crazy at times. I also know that my boys are called by God to do great things. God knows the plans He has for them, plans to prosper them, and not to harm them, plans to give them hope and a future (my paraphrase from Jeremiah 29:11). Even though I feel crazy and more tired than words can tell, I know that my boys are absolutely wonderful! All mothers of adorable kids are crazy for a time. Though I'm unsure how I'll nurse Joshua for his first year *and* go back to counselling and teaching, somehow, God will work it out and things will be fine. Though I'm unsure how we'll make our payments with Glen in school, God will also take care of this. He always pulls through. This season of craziness will pass, and soon another season will be upon me. I will wade through dirty dishes; "Krispies" will fall from my bare feet as I walk and rock my baby and dodge toy cars, trucks, and an assortment of clean and dirty laundry. I will follow Mary's example and learn to accept God's peace in life, no matter what the situation. Like Mary, I will walk confidently and joyfully, though dead tired because I choose to obey God. I will treasure each moment of craziness because no mother could be more blessed than I.

Chapter Three

Feeding Time at the Zoo

Each day in our family there is a "crabby" time of day for our toddler, Donovan. I now know what parents, who have gone before, mean when they say of their child, "He's 2." They say it with this ominous, helpless look on their faces and with their hands thrown up in mock protest. My 2-year-old Donovan, though incredibly delightful, fun, and highly energetic, also has his moments. No matter what I say or do within those moments, it's just not right. Donovan has always had a pattern with his outbursts—when he's tired or hungry. Being a clever mother, I have followed the advice of generations before that dealt with this malady—I feed him or put him to bed! The tricky part is figuring out how to navigate Joshua's ever-changing schedule into the overall plan of the day.

It seems that now all three of us get hungry at the same time, but Joshua needs nursing, while Donovan and I need cookies. Oh, I mean "real food." This would not be a problem if I were a highly organized mother. Joshua would be fed at precisely 4:30 P.M. Food would be in the oven and waiting for Glen, Donovan, and me at precisely 5:00 P.M. so we could avert the major hunger pain crisis for Donovan. We could all move to the already set table to partake of a wonderful meal where all happy people could share the events of the day. It would be a meal where everyone, including Donovan, would rave over the exquisite taste of the simple, yet delicious, food. A meal where all go away satisfied.

My reverie is interrupted by what actually happened as opposed to my well-laid plan! When 1:00 P.M. rolled around, Donovan had to wait for his nap because I was busy nursing Joshua; 2:00 P.M. and a tired Donovan was laid to rest in his crib—after having spilled a bag of salt all over the floor, table, and chairs. As I cleaned up the salt with the vacuum, Joshua screamed at the top of his little, though hearty, lungs.

He had pooped his diaper full and did not like it. Knowing he has a highly sensitive bottom, I made sure everything else was out of Donovan's reach and got some fresh water for the ten-minute diaper change. It takes a full ten minutes to change Joshua's diaper. Otherwise, his sensitive bottom becomes bright red with a rash. He is allergic to his acidic urine, and his little baby bottom has to be washed thoroughly and dried completely before pouring the cornstarch on and fastening a clean diaper.

While I was stuck at the changing table, cooing and smiling with Joshua, I heard nothing from Donovan. Hearing nothing from a toddler is rather scary, so I try to speed the bottom-drying process by blowing on Joshua—an act he finds quite hilarious. Finally, we get back to Donovan and discover the reason for his quietness. He's found the Rice Krispies—his favorite cereal. The Rice Krispies have found the floor, the chairs, and a tiny pile on the table. Donovan sits on a "big" chair with a huge grin on his face and says, "Krispies, Mom." I sigh and giggle a little.

Though it is more work for me, still on the same three hours of sleep, he seems so proud of himself for getting his own snack that all I can do is acknowledge his independence and say, "I see. Maybe next time you can ask Mommy for help, okay Sweet Pea?"

Donovan has finally started sleeping two hours straight in the afternoon, so he sleeps until 4:00 P.M. After two hours of playing, cooing, singing, and the classic "walking and rocking," Joshua finally falls asleep—at 3:55 P.M. I gently lay Joshua down in his bed and do the proverbial "backing" away from his cradle. You know, the one that the parenting books say not to do. I make a fast track for Donovan, who is getting louder and louder by the minute. After a quick diaper change, we run downstairs to play so Joshua has a small chance of sleeping longer. By 4:25 P.M., I have raced up the stairs to defrost some ground beef for hamburgers and raced back down to play with Donovan at least five times. By 4:26 P.M., Joshua has finished his famous Hildebrandt "Power Nap." In the nap department, Joshua is definitely taking after Grandpa Hildebrandt, who has been known to nap on the floor, behind the couch, or even on the floor in the middle of the hall but only for his ten-minute power nap! I leave Joshua in his crib for a few minutes in the vague hope that he may fall asleep again. When his wails become screams, I give in and bring him downstairs to "play." Donovan is not impressed that he has to share Mommy so soon, and the whining to watch "Bob and Larry" (Veggie Tales) begins.

By this time, Glen gets home from his trucking job; it is 6:30 P.M. We have finally sat down to a meal of the regular hamburgers, rice, and vegetables. Donovan is still whimpering because he wanted to watch *Veggie Tales Silly Songs* three times, not just once. He's decided that he's not going to eat. Joshua is crying to be held. Being hypoglycemic and not having eaten enough all day because of the obvious lack of time, I am shaky, starting to become irrational, and shoveling food into my mouth before something irrational comes out! I soon feel better, even though I still cannot hear because of the 1½ hours of loud wails. Donovan is convinced to eat and soon produces smiles, becoming his lovable, fun self once again.

A few things happened during this time. First, I pledged—again—to have supper ready by at least 5:30 P.M. Second, and more importantly, a strong lesson was learned. The thought struck me how dependent our bodies are on the daily sustenance of food. If we do not fuel our bodies regularly, we become shaky, irrational, and downright cranky. As adults, we can control the overwhelming urge to whine for awhile, but 2-year-olds have not yet mastered that mind/body control. Our daily food is as important to our bodies health as our daily intake of God is to our spiritual health. When we do not have our daily spiritual fuel, we become weak. Our minds lose their focus and clarity. God seems far away, even unreachable. We start to wonder if God really loves us, or if God can even love us when we do not keep in daily communion with Him.

When we do keep up our spiritual fuel intake, we do not doubt that God is there. We know God loves us because we are His precious children, heirs to His great kingdom. Though our backgrounds are different and varied, the truth of the Scriptures ring as true today as the day they were written. John 3:16 says, "For God so loved the world that He gave His only Son, that whoever believes in Him might have eternal life."

The message of God is love. God loves us plain and simple. He created us to love and be loved. Though we may distort our view of God and His love for us through lack of spiritual fuel, poor spiritual examples that have gone before us, or any multitude of lies that we may be believing, the truth of God's unconditional love for us is there. All we need to do is accept God's love, live as though we are loved by God, and fuel our spiritual body with the greatest food ever given to mankind, Jesus. Pass the greatest gift of love given by Jesus on to our children, along with a good dose of food, exercise, and sleep, and we have a well-balanced, well-fueled, happy family!

Chapter 4

Super-Mom

I sit in my backyard in total amazement. The sun is shining brightly down from a brilliantly blue sky. My bedding is washed and hanging on the dry rack. The kiddy-pool water lays in still peace on top of the soft, green grass. The swings hang idly. The sandbox sits untouched. Donovan and Joshua are actually both sleeping at the same time, and though I could be doing a multitude of household chores, I choose to soak in the autumn sunshine before the rain falls. I have discovered that mothers rarely just sit. I am taking a rare moment and just sitting, reflecting, contemplating life, and sipping my smoothie drink. It is wonderful.

My mind wanders to the life of a Dad. As I am not a Dad, I do not understand fully what it is like to be a Dad. I know that when I was growing up my Dad was my hero. Dad would go off to work in the morning, come home for supper in the evening, and then on many evenings, leave again for church meetings. As he was the pastor, this was simply the norm for our household. Yet he seemed to make time for us kids too. He would read to us, play with us, help us with our pets, and almost every evening he would look at me with a big grin and say, "How about some chocolate ice cream?"

I really can't imagine how he found time to be with us. Because Dad's time with us was shorter, I enjoyed it even more. I would "help" him with anything he allowed—fixing fences, shingling a roof, sawing wood, even hoeing the thousands of trees that we planted on our Saskatchewan acreage. If Dad said something it held weight because his integrity on and off the job was intact. I became fiercely protective of my Dad and was ready to fight anyone who said anything negative—except that pastors' daughters weren't allowed to fight!

Dad's role seemed to be intact. He was the provider and the hero. Growing up without a Dad would have been difficult. Only with God's strength could I imagine it possible. In contrast to my Dad, my mother was the one who was the constant. Though trained as a nurse, she chose to stay home with us three kids, only going back to work when we were teenagers. I realize now what a daunting task that must have been at times!

We had made various moves to various locations that must have worried both Mom and Dad, yet they were a constant source of love and affirmation in my life. Because she was the constant, Mom became the one who inflicted the discipline. Because I was a sensitive child, all I needed was a look, and I felt incredibly bad and never did the "bad" thing again. One vivid memory of my mother, which stands out in my memory, is the long walks she took with us kids.

One particular walk was on a sunny, spring afternoon near our acreage in Manitoba. The nearby river was always our destination spot because it held fascination beneath its murky, powerful surface. On this particular walk, my dog Sport suddenly slipped into a treacherous part of the river. The current did not pull him downstream, but he could not get out because of the steep embankment on all sides. As my older sister, younger brother, and I panicked, my mom simply got down on her stomach amidst the muck and grime of the river, told us to stand back, and single-handedly lifted a medium-sized dog out of the water. Perhaps my memory makes it seem more heroic, but this memory held in my mind as an amazing feat, and Mom became much more than just "Mom." She was my hero too. She was always there, and I knew beyond any doubt that my Mom would do much more for me than she had for our beloved dog.

Both parents were important to me as a child, and both are important to me now. Though their roles intermingle, it seems that both played different "tunes" in my growing up years. As I am now a Mom, I tried to put the two roles together in my mind so that I could make sense of them. What does a Mom or Dad role really look like?

My theory used to be that men simply neither would nor could ever understand what it is like to be a mother because they are not the "constant." Working Dads don't have to deal with the minute trials of every day nor the minute joys of every day. With this theory in mind, my thoughts turned to what it really means to be a mother.

When I look at my life and the life of my mother, a few things stand out. Ideally, mothers have to constantly be rational, loving human beings, even while putting up with crying, whining, and tears for any given number of hours each day. Mothers have to put their husbands as first priority, second only to God. She selflessly takes care of his needs and the children's needs.

After hearing crying for ten to thirty minutes, my husband amazingly retreats downstairs or finds an errand to do. Don't get me wrong—Glen is an absolutely incredible and wonderful husband and father. Because of his wonderfulness, I found myself becoming more and more chagrined each time he "retreated" after being home only briefly. I decided to ask around a bit—discreetly. What do other husbands do? I wanted to understand his position. I wanted to look at him with graciousness and compassionately attack my chagrin *and* his retreats. I soon discovered that other husbands—wonderful, loving husbands and fathers—do the same thing! This mystery was becoming almost annoying.

One evening I went to a friend's house for a bit, leaving our sleeping toddler, Donovan, and 11-week-old, awake Joshua with Glen. I vaguely registered his look of terror and pleading voice saying, "Be back in an hour!"

No watch on my wrist, a song in my heart, and freedom in my step, I bounded out the door and to the car. Having a lovely visit with my friend, I returned home one and a half hours later with a DQ blizzard for Glen. I walked into a *loud* room; Joshua was wailing with all the muster his little lungs could give. He was hungry. Glen was just plain angry. You have to understand; Glen does not get angry. "He's been crying for half an hour," he said and handed Joshua to me.

My "compassionate" reaction back, "Now you know what I go through everyday."

"But at least you can do something about it," Glen retorted as I quieted Joshua and then nursed him.

I contemplated this reply for a long while and later discussed it with Glen and a few trusted friends, with Glen's approval. I discovered that Glen and his friends actually believed that mothers have super powers. A mother's milk is perceived as the "power juice" that can quiet the most forceful wails. A mother's presence is seen as a soothing balm for calm, to prevail when food is not what is needed. A mother's arms are powerful and strong to hold her child for hours, yet soft and gentle to the touch. A mother's hands have mythical powers as they perform so many tasks—a gentle, comforting rub on the head, picking up endless toys, calming multiple children, washing never-ending dishes and laundry, changing diapers, doubling as a pacifier for babies desperate to suck anything—yet those same hands stay young, soft, and sexy for her man. Her lips are incredible wonders for they yield healing powers in their kiss. When delivered with a mother's love, a kiss from a mother's lips can heal multiple "owies." A mother's reflexes are at the speed of light to rescue her child from numerous dangers that occur throughout each day. She is light and nimble on her feet, and therefore, she never stumbles when holding several children and wading through mass amounts of toys on the floor. A mother does not feel physical pain. Therefore, when she's physically ill, everything is still taken care of on a household level. A mother's instincts are clear and quick. *Protect my family at all costs.* A mother needs little sleep to function well. Food is a mere trifle that is made for the sustenance of others, but rarely eaten by a mother; she is too busy getting up and down from the table to eat.

Though my description may be exaggerated a little, mothers are perceived as "Super Heroes." In contrast, fathers generally perceive themselves as "helpless" in the realm of the daily home routine.

This understood, I tried to dispel the myth and discuss the truth with Glen. The truth, though we hate to admit it, is that mothers are not super heroes. We do not own red tights and a cape imprinted with SUPER MOM. Sometimes the power juice causes colic instead of calm. Sometimes a mother's presence is not required for a peaceful atmosphere. Sometimes on the lullabies, a mother's voice falters and gets hoarse and croaks—from repeating fifty times a day to a 2-year-old, "No, you can't watch another video." Sometimes even a mother's kiss is not enough to soothe a painful hurt. And sometimes, all a mother wants to do is escape into her super hero husband's strong, powerful arms. Lulled into peace and confidence, she knows that it's okay if she did not meet the requirements of "Super Mom" that day.

I discovered a few important lessons through this theorizing process. I realized that my theory of "fathers never understanding mothers" was not quite accurate. We simply walk in different shoes. I found out that fathers think quite highly of mothers and their apparent high tolerance for noise—without completely losing their minds. Primarily, I discovered that although mothers and fathers can view each other as super heroes, when there is true love and acceptance, we can also acknowledge and fully accept the weaknesses we each have. Mothers and fathers both feel helpless at times—at a loss as to which step to take next. When those faltering steps of motherhood and fatherhood are taken together, they become the strong glue of parenthood.

Parenthood, standing together in love for each other and for our children, is the best gift we can give to our children—and the best gift we can give to each other. Though we play different parts, we can make a wonderfully harmonious song that blends beautifully into parenthood. For the sake of sanity, for Donovan and Joshua, and for each other, we choose to accept this gift from God. We choose parenthood as we forge ahead into this vast frontier.

Chapter Five

A Mother's Milk–
A Metaphor for Selfless Giving

On many days, it feels as if all I do is nurse Joshua—a physically draining process that makes me feel lifeless, lethargic, cuddly, and completely sleepy by the end. If it were not for the gnawing hunger in my stomach and the nagging thirst it creates, I would have a hard time moving from the nursing position into the diaper changing position, which is understandably what comes next! Nursing is something I have chosen for each of my boys because of its benefit for them. A mother's milk can help a child ward off sickness because of the immunities given through the milk. It has the potential to alleviate allergies later in life, before they begin. Again, it is because of the wonderful immunities being given. Psychologically, it is also very important to try to nurse your babies because of the unique bond that it creates between parent and child. It is a bond that I want to create and nurture throughout my boys' entire lives.

When I was pregnant, I was quite sick throughout the entire two pregnancies, sleeping very little because of the intense pain and sickness. I also developed more allergies than I already had, leaving me with few options for food. Yet in spite of all of this, except for Joshua's fairly severe colic and a few allergies, Donovan and Joshua seem to be quite healthy at this point in time. My theory, distorted though it may be, is that I gave up all of my immunity to them and bore the brunt of any sickness or allergy that may have come along.

Now, through nursing, I am doing the same sort of giving. I am, in many senses, tied to a nursing schedule. This implies the need to give up any personal schedule I may have had. When nursing, I give up a regular work schedule. Instead, I counsel my clients around Joshua's nursing schedule. I also give up some time with friends. Physical workouts are hard on the milk supply, so I must give them up, or curtail them to be shorter so that my milk supply is not used up. I even give up taking certain medication that could help the intense headaches that I have regularly. I give up herbal cleansing programs to get my body back into a healthier mode. I give up sleep so that my baby is well-fed and happy—especially in the first few months when he needs to eat more often.

Motherhood and breast-feeding are full of giving. Wise words from my chiropractor ring through my head, "A mother's milk—a metaphor of selfless giving." In many ways, this is true, yet it causes me to do some introspection. How often do I look longingly on the other side of the fence? How selfless is that when given grudgingly?

As I gaze down at my nursing baby boy, my eyes swell with tears of joy. A lump forms in my throat. A smile plays at my lips. A mother's love is incomprehensible. Never before have I loved so fully and so deeply. It is not the romantic love that grows through nurturing in marriage. It is not the love of two close friends. It is a mother's love. It is pure, simple, unconditional. It is selfless giving, never expecting anything in return. It is full and warm. It encompasses one's whole being with a powerful force that is selfless. It is a love that fiercely, yet gently, protects. This love says, "No one touches my children."

This love reminds me of our Heavenly Father's love for us. Selfless. Giving. Fiercely, yet gently protecting. John 3:16 states, "For God so loves the world that He gave His only Son, that whoever believes in Him will not perish but have everlasting life."

God gave his *Son* to die for us, his *children!* Wow! Talk about giving up things for kids. God gave up Jesus to death on a cross—the worst possible kind of death—for us rebellious kids whom He loves *so much!* Jesus fought the fight for us. He bore the brunt of our sins so that we do not have to—just as a mother would rather get sick than watch her children suffer—yet on a much larger scale! Jesus rose victorious so that when we do give Jesus our sins, our shame, our hurts, and our pain, He can bear them because the fight is already fought.

In Matthew 23:37, the Father's love is compared to a mother hen gathering her chicks protectively under her wings. Since becoming a mother, I am now able to comprehend slightly more God's incredible love for us, His children. This understanding is not complete yet, as it will be when I get to Heaven. It is growing to an amazing comprehension that simply says "Wow!" at the presence of the Lord of Hosts.

This understanding gives me another glimpse into the character of God. God's love for us is simple. He cannot help but love us because we are His kids, His creation. We are formed in the very image of God as Genesis states. God gave us souls and formed every sinew of us. We have incredible worth because God gives us incredible worth and gives us the privilege of being called sons and daughters of God, heirs to a royal priesthood, with a specific plan for each one of us.

God's love for us is pure and unconditional. There are no strings attached. He loves us unconditionally, no matter what we have done. He expects nothing from us for Him to give His love. Just as a mother, He is grieved when we do not want to spend time with Him. Just as a mother, He is saddened when we do not love Him back. Just as a mother, His love is not contingent on whether or not we love Him or spend time with Him. He loves us, His children, regardless of who we are or what we do. He compares us to no one.

God's love for us is full and warm. Its power knows no bounds. God's love can melt rock-hard hearts. God's love can break strong chains that hold people in bondage to a life of darkness and sin, offering them complete and total freedom in His love. God's love is a love that does not bind, but rather leads for those willing to follow. For those who are willing to follow, God's love pours out incredible blessings too wonderful even to comprehend. God's love brings incredible light and brightness into a black night. God's love is gentle and caring. He will never do something for us if we do not willingly want it because God is the ultimate gentleman. It saddens God when we do not want the blessings that He has to offer us, but He will never impose Himself or His love upon us. God's love is simply there for the taking.

God loved us enough to send his Son through a mortal woman, Mary. I sometimes wonder what it was about Mary that enabled her to become the mother of Jesus. She must have been an incredible woman—one whom I can't wait to meet when I get to heaven. With the selfless description of what Mothers strive to be and considering who Jesus and God the Father are, I picture Mary as a quiet, giving, selfless woman of God. I think she was of strong character to withstand the pressures that she must have faced for bearing what looked to the entire world as an "illegitimate" child. From all accounts, she simply and quietly stood her ground and was not swayed from what she knew to be from God. Her faith in God the Father was constant. Her love for God was pure and unconditional. She seemingly showed no doubts. Mary gave up much of her reputation for God, in order to bear the Son of God. She understood what a great privilege it was. Mary seemed to see the big picture of who God is and realized that life on earth is only but a chapter of eternity.

God also gave up much for us, His children. May I have the humbleness of heart to accept God's love and grace in my life, so that I can give it freely and without reserve to my children. May God grant me the grace to see the big picture of eternity as opposed to just the here and now so that I can give selflessly to my children, not just now, but always. God started this legacy of love at the beginning of time. Mary continued the legacy of love with the birth of Jesus. Jesus continued the legacy of love by dying for us on the cross and rising victorious so that we can inherit eternal life in Christ. Let the legacy of love continue through the heart of a mother. Let this legacy of love continue through me to my precious children.

Chapter 6

Treasure the Moments

Today I realized that my toddler, my 2-year-old, my little sweet pea, my oldest child, is growing up—fast! We are at my in-laws' new house in Alberta for Christmas, where much action takes places on a regular basis. Today the cousins were over, which is always cause for excitement in Donovan's mind. Watching Donovan's joyful play with his older cousins brought many giggles to me and my relatives. As I took a break from the excitement and retired into the quietest place I could find in order to nurse Joshua, Donovan came striding in with strength of step and confidence in his eyes. "Hi, Mom."

Hi, Mom? That was the big phrase that caught me off guard. Donovan talks a lot; he has said "Hi, Mom" often. This time seemed different. The light in his eyes. The confidence. The strength. It all said, "I'm growing up now, Mom. I still need you so I just came to see if you're still around. Now that I know you're here and okay, I can run to you in time of need, I can go back and play with the other kids."

Of course, this is my interpretation of the brief, yet so precious interaction that transpired between us. My heart melted with his words. Love filled me to the brim of my tired, swollen eyes. The thought that caught me off guard was that *my Donovan is growing up.*

The list of things that make me know he's growing up continues to expand. Suddenly, I don't have to know where he is every second, and I can trust him more with not getting into too many things (at least not too many for a 2-year-old). He has most of his toddler Bible almost memorized—he knows exactly which story comes next and is mortally offended if it's not read to him. He prayed for people tonight and reminds me to pray. He runs in from the midst of "play-land" imagination and says, "Hi, Mom." Then he turns to Joshua and says, "Hi, Cootie." ("Cutie" would be the interpretation of that one!) He wants to "help" with everything! He has even started putting his toys away on occasion whether asked or not. He took his medicine three times today on a spoon without too much fuss! (Although I did put a couple of "Smarties" on the spoon to help it down—worked like a charm!)

Despite the evidence of maturity, there are actions from Donovan that say loud and clear to me, "I'm still two, and don't you forget it!" For instance, the tears when things don't go his way. The way he can't possibly sit still in church through more than one or two songs. We sing at least ten to twelve in our church, so this makes singing a challenge for me and sitting for Donovan even more of a challenge! There is also the way he still needs me to stay with him in the nursery at church. "Mom, stay. Mom, sit," as he takes my hand and leads me to a chair. The way he gets into many things, like the Christmas tree decorations that continually are taken down. The oats, sugar, and cereal also keep finding their way to the floor for some mysterious reason. I'm also recalling the cups that keep getting rearranged in different cupboards, in the toy box, or on the floor!

One day Donovan and Joshua were quite teary eyed. Joshua was crying the loudest, while I courageously kept trying to make supper. Finally, after about a minute or two of loud crying, which is about all my ears and heart can stand, I stopped supper preparations and picked up Joshua. I looked at Donovan and said, "Joshua needs some attention."

Donovan looked up at me with his wide, blue eyes and said in utter seriousness, "Donvan need tension too." (Interpretation: Donovan needs attention too.) My heartstrings certainly were pulled! Glen came home to see all three of us cuddling on the kitchen floor.

These events again cause me to reflect on life and what is important in life. How important is supper preparation or trying to keep the house perfect (which is impossible with small children), in comparison to giving my children all the attention that I can? Of course, certain things need to be done in order to successfully run a household so that we don't go crazy with the chaos of mess. Yet even more important things need to be done in order to successfully run a home and raise kids—kids that will in turn use our example to raise their own children. In the book of Luke, it says that Mary "treasured all these things in her heart." What does it mean to treasure? How can we treasure each moment and hold it in our hearts? How can it stay there amidst the worries, joys, and busyness of each and every day?

According to the Oxford Canadian Dictionary, treasure means "wealth or riches stored or accumulated, especially in the form of gems, precious metals; a hoard of such wealth; a thing valued for its rarity, workmanship, associations; a much loved or highly valued person; value highly; cherish, prize; store for preservation or future use."[1] This means that I must value my children and the experiences with them above all. Prioritizing my children in the biblical order, which I understand to be God first, husband second, children third, then church, extended family, and other stuff in life. If I treasure my children and treasure the moments, I will value those moments while in the moment and out of the moment.

There are some moments that I love so much that I never want them to end. I wish that time would simply stand still while I am in those moments so that I can never forget what they are like. Moments like holding my boys, watching them have new experiences, witnessing their love for God grow as we pray, and witnessing to them the wonders of who He is. There are also moments I want to lose, and I want them to leave my memory—moments like my voice sounding louder and harsher than I would like with my boys—moments where I would rather not be home with my boys, but rather out for a break! Unfortunately, the human brain has a tendency to remember the harsh moments more than the positive moments. It takes seven compliments to undo one harsh word, and we'll still have the harsh word experience stronger in our memories. In spite of this, we do remember everything that happens to us. Psychology teaches that our bodies and brains are so incredibly wired that we actually have body memories for those that our brains "seem" to have forgotten. We cannot actually forget things; our brains just file them somewhere that is labeled "unimportant to me right now—so inaccessible file."

In most cases, remembering everything is a good thing. The filing system needs to change. In Philippians 4:8 Paul says, "Finally, brothers, whatever is true, whatever is noble, whatever is right, whatever is pure, whatever is lovely, whatever is admirable—if anything is excellent or praiseworthy—think about such things." Treasuring the moments with our children is doing just that. We can choose to file the wonderful memories in the "keep forever" file and have those memories influence our ebb and flow of life, until a lifetime of positive memories and a storehouse of treasure is accomplished. With those moments that we would rather lose, we can choose to learn from them and change our thoughts and behavior the next time. Sometimes that simply takes a conscious effort on our part; sometimes it takes asking for help from someone else, but even us creatures of habit can change and be healed. With this treasuring being done, we can choose to be like Mary and "treasure" the moments.

Although my boys are growing up, they are still very little and will always need me in some way. My role, throughout the years, will change as their needs change. My guess is that no matter how grown up they get, if I give freely of my time, my love, and "tension" (attention) now while they still want and ask for it, they will grow up healthy, happy boys. They will have a storehouse of treasures gifted to them, in the form of memories given to them by Glen and myself.

May God grant me the purity of heart to be a model of God's love to Donovan and Joshua. May I be a vessel for God in raising them. May I always, like Mary, treasure each and every moment in my heart.

Chapter 7

Keep Your Eyes on Mommy

Today was Joshua's first bath in the "big" tub. The baby tub was just too small for my growing boy. Every move he made, which was many, was followed by a squeal of delight and a wave of water washing over the side onto me, the floor, the bathroom counter, and basically everything in reach. Joshua's every encounter with the baby tub meant there would be a lake on the floor. It did not take too many lakes on the floor before I decided it was time for the big tub.

Holding Joshua on my lap, I balanced myself on the side of the tub and started filling the clean bathtub with nice, warm bath water. Hearing water splashing he leaned over to take a look. Joshua glanced up at me with his wide, blue eyes filled with utter curiosity; a smile spread across his entire face. This looked like fun to him! Now my bouncing baby boy was balanced over my leg and arm with me holding tightly to him, lest he, the baby with no fear, decided to dive for the water!

Turning off the water, I lifted the already naked Joshua close to me for a dry hug before his encounter with the new world of bathing. I whispered to him softly as he cooed into my ear and grabbed hold of my hair with his strong baby hands, yanking my head wherever he happened to want it. Gently pulling him far enough away from me to look into his face, I slowly leaned down and placed him into a sitting position within the bathtub. A look of sheer terror crossed through his eyes as I eased him down into a lying position in the tub. I positioned my left arm securely under his neck and head to keep his face above water. He looked from side to side of the green tub then let out a little whimper. My fearless baby was definitely showing fear!

"Joshua," I gently called directing his attention back to me. His eyes stopped looking around him as they slowly focused on my eyes. My heart overflowed with love for my baby as I gently talked to him. "Just keep your eyes on Mommy, Joshua, and everything will be okay. You're okay, Sweetheart," I coaxed as I washed him with a soft, baby face cloth. "Just keep your eyes on Mommy, and you'll be just fine."

Joshua smiled as he looked at me. As long as I kept talking and he kept looking at me, his fear was gone. When he looked away, the fear came back. Soon his bath was complete, and he was wrapped in his hooded towel, securely in my arms for more cuddles.

I smiled as a favorite story from my childhood days came back to me. "Read me the story about Jesus walking on the water, Mom," I would say almost every night as we picked up the *God Keeps His Promises* book for a story. I loved and still love how Jesus walked out onto the water to meet the disciples in the dead of a blustery night. I can't help but think how scared the disciples must have been. Matthew 14:26 says, *"When the disciples saw him walking on the lake, they were terrified. 'It's a ghost,' they said, and cried out in fear."*

When I was a child, it was easy to say, "But Mom and Dad, how come they thought that Jesus was a ghost after all the miracles He did? Didn't they recognize Him?" Maybe it is still a legitimate question. Yet many times we live in fear, and we do not recognize our Lord coming out to reassure us, to cuddle us, and hold us safe and secure in his strong arms. We, like most of the disciples, recoil in fear and sink into ourselves, unable to move because the fear is so great.

Yet one of Jesus' first disciples stands out more than the rest. Peter. The rock. Peter, though frightened too, does not recoil. He hears Jesus' voice calling out to him above the waves of the storm. Matthew 14:27 says, *"But Jesus immediately said to them: "Take courage! It is I. Don't be afraid."* Calming words—spoken from the One who can deliver real peace in the midst of our storm. "Don't be afraid. It is I, Jesus." How often we don't hear these calming words above the terror of our own hearts, and the fear that need not be there.

Peter was different. He was a man built like a rock. He was relatively fearless. Yet even Peter doubted a bit. He tested Jesus to make sure that it was really Him, just like I often tend to do. "Lord," I pray, "if this is really what you want me to do, give me a great sign."

Peter calls back to His Lord. Matthew 14:28 says, *"Lord, if it's you,"* Peter replied, *"tell me to come to you on the water."*

Here is the part I love best. There is absolutely no hesitation on Peter's end. He simply obeys. Would I do the same? Do I truly do the same? Do I simply obey Jesus—who doesn't have to prove Himself again and again? He answers, "Yes, Laurel, it is me. And yes, I do want you to do this."

Matthew 14:29–32 finishes this incredible story. *"Then Peter got down out of the boat, walked on the water and came toward Jesus. But when he saw the wind, he was afraid and, beginning to sink, cried out, "Lord, save me!" Immediately Jesus reached out his hand and caught him. "You of little faith,"* he said, *"why did you doubt?"*

And when they climbed into the boat, the wind died down. Then those who were in the boat worshipped him, saying, "Truly you are the Son of God."

As long as Peter kept his eyes fixed on Jesus, walking on water was easy. As soon as he started to look around at the storm, at the water that he was miraculously walking upon, and at the surrounding circumstances, fear crept in, leaving no room for faith in God to keep him afloat. Fortunately, Peter was smart and did still have a fair amount of faith. He had enough faith to realize that Jesus was on the water with him. He had enough faith to realize that if he didn't call out for help to the only one who could save him, he was going to sink into the murky depths of his fear and not succeed at the task at hand. So he called out for Jesus to help him before he sunk too deep into his fear and forgot that Jesus was there to save him.

I think that Jesus' admonishment to Peter was as gentle as it is to us. "Why did you doubt?" Jesus asked as He efficiently rescued Peter, and us, from the miry depths. Jesus' ways are gentle and loving. His intent is never to create fear, for perfect love casts out fear (1 John 4:18), and Jesus' love is pure and perfect. Oh, for the faith of a child like my Joshua whose trust in me is implicit, complete, and perfect, for he has been given no reason not to trust me.

The question that naturally comes to my mind is simple. Were we ever given a reason not to trust completely in God? I do know that some think that they have been given reasons not to trust Jesus. Friends have "backstabbed" them. They have been abused, some quite severely, by strangers, friends, and even family. Where was Jesus? As a counsellor, I get this question quite regularly. I think that sometimes the answer lies in where we are or where we are looking. Where was Peter looking when he started to fear? He was looking away from Jesus. Jesus didn't leave him standing on the water by himself. He was right there in front of Peter, giving him courage and allowing him to do something that is simply not humanly possible. The point is that Jesus was right there. When we have troubles, no matter how big or small, Jesus is right there. When I get the question in counselling sessions, "Where was Jesus?" I don't give an answer. Instead, if my clients are willing, I suggest that they ask Jesus that question. The answer is always a similar variation of "I was right there with you. I was hurting with you. I was the one crying at your bedside, angry at the atrocities you were receiving, weeping with you, holding you, and giving you strength. I was right there."

Apart from some health problems, I have been incredibly blessed in life. I haven't been given a single reason not to trust God. His faithfulness to my family and me is complete and full, perfect and pure. He always provides a way. I simply need to trust and obey; the blessings will follow. The obey part always includes a continued molding of my character to becoming more Christ-like. When I do surrender to being molded then blessings do indeed follow. God's blessings are so exciting—like metaphorically walking on the water, like the love I give and receive from my family, like the majestic gift of a sunset—straight from the hand of the artist! I am excited to "walk on the water" with Jesus and to witness more of God's incredible power. I am excited to worship God and proclaim with the disciples, "Truly you are the Son of God!" I am excited to impart this faith on to my children. I am excited to learn from them the childlike faith that comes from complete trust in a God who never fails. May I keep my eyes on Jesus so that I can walk fearlessly ahead on the murky waters—while being a warrior for God and an example for my children.

Chapter 8

Late Again

"Be still and know that I am God." Psalm 46:10

I don't know about other mothers, but I am always late wherever I go, no matter how hard I try! It is the most frustrating thing in the entire world—especially in the middle of the lateness. It is also difficult for my husband, an otherwise patient and understanding man, who loses his cool when we are late for things such as church, doctors' appointments, friends, etc.! Actually, "difficult" is a mild term to describe the pain and agony of being late for Glen. He grew up in a family that was never late. They considered being five minutes early the equivalent of being late. I consider being five minutes early good timing! Before kids, I was actually starting to make it to places on time, with a considerable and conscious effort on my part. Now . . . well . . . I'm not only back to square one, I've gone into the negative side of the squares! Let me illustrate my point.

The day starts out seemingly fine as Joshua and Donovan wake me promptly at 8:00 A.M.—oblivious to the three night feedings that last one or two hours each (because Joshua struggles with colic). I am not a morning person, and I must point out that 8:00 A.M. is actually early and still a groggy time of day. I groan, roll out of bed, stumble to the living room (which for now is Joshua's room until he can sleep consistently through the night and share a room with Donovan), pick up either a happy or crying baby, and stumble back to the refuge of my warm bed to nurse Joshua. He latches on and eats with great hunger, while I lean my head on the cold, hard wall and let my bloodshot, swollen eyes droop closed. He finishes eating and throws himself backward after a brief five to ten minutes, looking up at me with his characteristic grin and sparkling blue eyes. I smile back at him, peering through the slits that have tried to stay open.

Donovan calls from his crib again, "Mommy, Mommy, Mommy! I wake up! MOMMY!" I haul my tired body out of bed and wonder why I still feel so tired. Still holding Joshua, my feet somehow find my slippers, and we are soon padding the few steps to Donovan's room. "Good morning, Donovan!" I muster as cheerfully as can. Donovan has been a real trooper waiting so long for me to get him out of bed. I am very proud of how patient he is with me while I care for Joshua. Smiling, I reach my free hand down to help him up. He promptly hands me everything in his crib. "And here's Boo-Boo and puppy and mommy elephant . . ." The list goes on until Joshua and I are both laden down with his treasures that must go with Donovan everywhere. Everything out of his crib, Donovan wraps his arms around my neck. Soon I am holding a 30 pound 2-year-old and a 20 pound 7-month-old. Feeling very fortunate, I kiss them both. I soon also feel very "heavy laden" and lower all three of us to the floor. Surrounding Joshua with toys, I quickly change Donovan's diaper. This process is surprisingly quick now after dealing with Joshua's ten-minute diaper changes. After Donovan has a clean "deeper" (as he calls it), it is time to select clothes for the day. This is inevitably a longer process. Being 2 means that Donovan is developing his independence . . . as if he wasn't before that! He has to select what to wear, including what socks to wear. It doesn't matter if it doesn't match. It doesn't matter how old it is. What matters is that he selects it. Fortunately, I don't have much sense of style so I don't usually care what he selects!

It's 9:00 A.M.; we're making good time. We've only been awake for an hour. Joshua still needs to get dressed and have a diaper change, but Donovan is hungry and getting grumpy. In fact, I'm hungry and getting grumpy! I make the suggestion to Donovan that he could eat while I change Joshua. It is met with outright disapproval from a determined 2-year-old, who runs into the living room to play with his farm animals. Deciding to choose my battles, I head into the bedroom to change Joshua. Now it's 9:20 A.M. Joshua is changed, and Donovan decides to get my clothes out for me too. He wants me to wear the cow shirt today. For someone who is 2, a shirt that is filled with Holstein cows and says "101 Cowmations" is very attractive. Knowing that my shirt will soon be full of all kinds of lovely slobber and food from their plates, I comply. While I put on my shirt, Donovan starts walking around my room looking for my pants. I shake my head and say, "It's okay Donovan. Mommy can do it. You don't have to take care of me." Characteristic of being 2, he selectively does not hear what I am saying but notices that I have already found my blue jeans. He nods in approval, smiling at me. "Mommy's pants," he grins. Shoving my bare feet back into my slippers, I pick up Joshua from the bed where he has been happily playing with Glen's hat and follow my quick Donovan into the kitchen.

The time is 10:00 A.M., and we are all in the kitchen. I have finally sat down to spoon some oatmeal into my mouth. Donovan has decided to eat half of my oatmeal because that is also a cool thing to do—eat whatever is on Mom's plate because it must be better than whatever is on his. In between mouthfuls, I feed Joshua his cereal. Joshua is already getting sleepy and ready for his morning nap. Again, we have missed the opportunity for a morning walk because we were too slow. I sigh.

Donovan looks up and grins at me. "Mommy tired?"

I smile and nod. "Yes, Sweetie. Mommy's tired, but I sure do love you!" He smiles and says loudly, "I love you too, Mommy!" What music to my ears!

But there seems to be some other music. Joshua is winding up the crying button and getting louder by the second.

Removing him from the high chair, I hold him close to me and whisper, "It's okay Josh. You're okay." Donovan joins in with me. "You're okay, Josh-u-a," he says concerned, enunciating every syllable.

Fifteen minutes later and I am giving Joshua his second diaper change; this one a bit smellier than the first. Singing lively songs helps him lie still for the process, so a giggling Joshua listens as I sing *Teensy Weensy Spider* and *Joshua and the Battle at Jericho,* with the appropriate silly faces to match the songs. In between songs and tickles, he whimpers and holds his legs up to his stomach giving me incredibly endearing looks. We cuddle for awhile, then I put him into his crib to go to sleep with the perpetual prayer of every mother on my lips, "Lord, please let him sleep! He is so tired!" I'm quite sure God hears this same prayer from all over the globe about 50 million times a day! Holding Donovan's hand, we go downstairs for him to catch *Sesame Park* on TV. I'm no advocate of TV, but I must admit that I sure am thankful for a few acceptable kids shows in the morning that give me some semblance of a break! Wanting to spend a bit of time just being with my boy, I snuggle in with Donovan. Before I blink, *Sesame Park* is over. Sighing, I shake my head at my lack of discipline to get up and shower or have my devotions or step on the Stairmaster.

"*Raccoons* coming, Mommy?" Donovan asks. He knows what shows come when.

"Yes, Sweetie," I answer. "The *Raccoons* are coming." I race quietly up the stairs, grab my Bible and shorts, and race back down again.

I change into shorts and jogging shoes, grab my Bible, and hop on the Stairmaster. Thirty seconds into a rousing workout, the phone rings. I sigh. Donovan looks up from the *Raccoons* and says, "Phone, Mommy!" I have to laugh. Kids have the cutest way of pointing out the obvious. Hopping down I jog to the office and answer the phone. It's a business call so five minutes later I'm back on the stair climber. The clock registers

11:45 A.M. so I can go for 15 minutes, read my Bible while working out, be with Donovan, and have a shower in the afternoon during nap time. The phone rings again. It's another business call, but this one is also a friend.

Fifteen minutes later, I am off the phone and Donovan is turning off the TV. What an amazing boy! "*Raccoons* all done, Mommy!"

"Wow!" I say as I scoop Donovan up and swing him high in the air. He giggles then runs into the office saying, "Ducks, Mommy!"

"There's no ducks in there Donovan! They're outside!" I try reasoning.

He points to the computer, again saying, "Ducks."

I finally clue in. Glen has downloaded a monster truck game onto the computer that Donovan loves to watch. Taking into consideration that Joshua is still sleeping, I take the bait and we play monster trucks together. Five minutes into our game, Joshua wakes up. Dragging a whining boy away from the computer, we go upstairs and get Joshua.

Soon I am rushing around the kitchen again. "Donovan," I try reasoning again, "Mommy and Joshua have a doctor's appointment this afternoon at 1:40. We have to hurry and eat so we'll make it there on time."

I'm never sure how much he actually understands, but he complies with an "Okay, Mom." Unfortunately, Donovan's compliance is merely verbal. He proceeds to cry about what he wants to eat for lunch, which bib he wants to wear, and which seat he wants to sit in. Finally, with a cheese honey sandwich in hand (which is basically what he would eat every meal if I allowed it) and wearing his "Pooh" and "Tigger" bib, Donovan is finally somewhat settled in his booster seat. He is still whining somewhat because he has a sippie cup instead of the fish cup from Red Robin's restaurant. To a two-year-old, drinking from a cup without a lid means that you can also dip your play elephant in and out of the liquid inside the cup–much to my dismay!

During the settling process of Donovan, Joshua is winding up again for a loud scream. Scooping him up, I tell Donovan that I'm going to feed Joshua. He nods. "Okay, Mom." Sitting in the living room to nurse Joshua, I carefully position myself within view of Donovan. It's already 1:00 P.M. I have no idea how it got to be so late. My spirits sink a little as I think about the shower that never happened. It's amazing how something as simple as a shower can get your hopes and spirits up! I look down at Joshua nursing and become mesmerized with my baby. Nothing matters anymore as my heart becomes full of the most incredible, all encompassing love for my child. I can't help but think what a miracle a baby is! The long nine months of sickness was worth it for my Joshua and my Donovan.

Too soon, Joshua is done nursing and grinning up at me. I glance at the clock. It is now 1:15 P.M.; I plot my course of action. I'll spoon food into Joshua, eat my noodles very quickly, and run and change. No problem.

The clock mocks me as it says 1:25 P.M. and sees me panicking and calling my parents who live down the street. My mom picks up the phone. "Help!" I say without identifying myself.

"What?" she sounds quite concerned and a bit confused.

"Help, Mom! It's Laurel. I have to be at the doctor by 1:40 and none of us are ready!" As I talk, I have already scooped Joshua up, and I'm changing his diaper. Mom and Dad have to go baby-sit at my sister's, but they decide to come, take Donovan, and meet me at the doctor's office. I quickly get ready then answer the door for my Dad.

"Grandpa!" Donovan is thrilled. Grandpa is his favorite person in the whole world. I sigh in relief then rush out the door to get Joshua settled into his car seat. It's 1:40 by the time I leave. I get to the bottom floor of where my doctor is located and impatiently wait for the slowest elevator in all of Abbotsford to come. Finally, at 1:55 P.M., I walk into the doctor's office and lower my eyes. I am fifteen minutes late. This is not good. It is embarrassing. "Sorry I'm late!" I apologize to the receptionist.

She only says, "What's your name?"

And so the day goes. My lateness causes others to be late—like my parents who stayed to help me. On other days, it's other people who are put out. I know that I am hard on myself, but I can't keep from wondering how other mothers make it to places on time and look good in the process! My doctor looked at me and said, "And how are you doing? Pushing yourself too hard as usual?" It's nice to know that someone knows me well enough to call me on my too high expectations of life!

Thinking about my own busy life causes me to reflect on Jesus' life. I wonder how Jesus did all that he did in such a short time here on earth. Of course, Jesus is 100 percent divine, yet while on earth he was also 100 percent human. He healed more than we are told about in the Scriptures. He spoke to so many. He touched many lives with His understanding, sincerity, compassion, and most of all, His love. Jesus' eyes must have been pools of love, reflecting the Father's great love for His children. I know that Jesus got tired because it says that He would go to the garden of Gethsemane and rest. Just rest. And there is the key to an abundant life. When Jesus says to follow Him, He means every step of the way, to seek to know Him better so that we *can* follow Him. We are to do his bidding, to have compassion on those around us, to love with sincerity, and to reach out to others. Yet it means much more than this! Jesus rested. That is when he talked to God, and more importantly, it is when he listened to God. Getting to know Jesus means that we need to rest and to sit still in order to hear his voice. We cannot hear the voice of God when we are running here and there, taking care of everyone, but missing God's instructions, his wise words that are meant just for us. So for busy mothers, who are involved in church and may also work outside the home, what exactly does this mean? One can't exactly drop everything when there are financial obligations. One can't ignore one's children—nor would one want to! My children are a gift from God and take incredible priority over everything else. I hate leaving them to go to work, even though I love my work as a counsellor.

For me to rest means to take advantage of the minutes I do have throughout each day and use them wisely. For example, it takes a brief five minutes to read my Bible every day. I would like more time than that; but with kids this little and even less sleep for my mind, five minutes is better than nothing! Praying with my kids is also a daily occurrence that happens often throughout each day. Seeing God in everything and communicating that, not only to my kids but also to God, is important in my relationship with Him. As Brother Lawrence wrote, I must "practice the presence of God" for He is always with me. To rest means to take time to sleep when I can. Resting means to be still before the Lord my God, the Maker of Heaven and earth. When I am still, then and only then, can I hear the Divine voice of God that leads me on. Maybe then, I will be on time if I keep working at it, implementing God's plan for my life.

Oh, my Father in Heaven, lead me on throughout each day!

Chapter 9

Too Tired to Enjoy the Blessings

By 10:00 A.M. this morning, the distinct drawling, country song about nobody knowing all the troubles that I've seen and the pain I have felt, except Jesus, was slurring through my tired brain. Joshua woke up with a cold, again. He had only been healthy for five days, and now here we go again. It is so hard on him to be sick, and I am so concerned that he is going to be like me—allergies on top of allergies—that I go into my worry mode. I get quieter than normal, even though I'm not an extraordinarily loud person. I have to look for things to laugh at. When Joshua cries, I get annoyed, then I get worried, and then I chastise myself for being both. Then Donovan starts into the whining mode or the no listening mode. It really doesn't matter which one he chooses because both of them annoy me, especially when I am in the worry mode.

When Joshua is sick, he goes into the cry mode. Joshua is just barely 9-months-old as I write this. He has been stuffed up most of his short life. He has had colic for eight months of this same life. Every tooth that has come in has caused a major upset in his poor, little body—such as fever and bleeding gums—all equaling a very sore mouth. Joshua to date has eight teeth and is currently working on more. I guess he may as well get them all in the same year as everything else! My doctor tells me that infants have six to eight colds in their first year because they are building up an immunity. Joshua must have an incredible immunity by now! Unfortunately this immunity has not decided to show itself in his sweet little life.

Joshua is such a fun-loving little boy. When he's sick, he just wants Mommy. Lately, I've been feeling like everyone wants a piece of me, and I'm running out of pieces to give, and I'm definitely running out of fuel! Donovan and Joshua have both needed to be held and quieted from abundant tears, at the same time, at least four times today. My husband has been away all day too. He is a full-time student, which is very good . . . and very bad. How do you tell people how you're doing when you're doing very good . . . and very bad? This is my dilemma lately. I've trained myself to be a very cognitive person, which is a good thing because I can talk myself into a good and healthy state of mind when I get into those worry modes. It is also a good thing because I am a counsellor and need to guide others into positive thinking. Yet I am so tired from the incredible lack of sleep that my brain is having a hard time functioning! When brain functions physically start to shut down because of an unfulfilled basic need, such as sleep . . . well . . . I have to work very hard to maintain a healthy, cognitive level of functioning.

I put Joshua down for his nap this morning at 10:30 A.M. because my arms were so tired from holding him, and he wouldn't stop crying. He promptly fell asleep, which is unusual for him, meaning he really wasn't feeling that great. Donovan wanted to play downstairs so I decided to wash the scum from my windows downstairs—a chore I have been "ordered" to do since a recent visit to the allergist. One window was halfway done by 12:00 P.M., when Joshua woke up again. Oh well. Washing the window was good therapy. I had a bit more energy and felt good about life. Joshua must surely be happier now. Donovan and I bounced up the stairs, only to find a disgruntled Joshua, who again was only happy if Mommy was holding him. In comes Grandma. I don't know what we would do without my parents living close by! She decided to come visit the boys, and I actually got to eat lunch in one sitting, a rare novelty. (Actually it didn't get accomplished in one sitting, but I only got up about six times as opposed to twenty times!)

Again, naptime came early in the afternoon for both boys. Donovan was actually quite happy to go to bed because he likes to "read" his books in bed. I think this is his quiet time away from a mommy who always wants to play with him! Joshua also went down earlier than normal and slept well. I promptly finished washing the window downstairs just in time for Donovan to wake up and want out of bed!

This is just a snippet from my day, but I must say that the day was trying. I could blame it on Joshua being sick, always wanting to be held, and crying incessantly. I could blame it on Donovan not listening to me and getting into the Vaseline, poking Joshua in the eye four times, or swinging around a stick ten times—after I told him no an equal amount of times. I could blame it on my body hurting all over from holding babies, lack of sleep, or strange beds. (Joshua has taken over our bedroom because he sleeps better there. We have moved downstairs to the living room.) I could even blame it on Glen for not being around enough to help and having an essay due tomorrow that he has not done. I won't even really see him when he walks through the door. Blame cannot be placed squarely on the shoulders of any of these problems. All of them together equal a life that is in the season of sleepless nights, crying, sick babies, and Vaseline everywhere. This season of life is called early parenthood, and I would dare to say that other mothers have similar trying days. Their brains have a hard time getting to the blessings. Some days I'm just too tired to enjoy the blessings that God has given me. These are the times when I must consciously look back and find each infinite blessing, no matter how big or small these blessings may be.

When I look back to the blessings of the day, I picture Donovan sitting on my lap, drinking his bottle, and talking with me. This is so precious to me, especially because he is such a busy boy. I love it when he cuddles on my lap. I see him with a big smile on his face as he walks out of his room covered in Vaseline—quite proud of himself. Vaseline is hard to get off, but it was quite funny! I see my Mom coming and feeding Joshua his lunch, changing his diaper, and playing with both of the boys on the living room floor while I finished my lunch. This is precious. Grandparents are so special. We are so blessed to have two sets of grandparents who love our children and want to spend time with them.

I see my husband Glen trying to rub some of the pain out of my neck, shoulders, back, and arms before heading off to the computer to work on his essay. I remember the moment of relaxation in Glen's arms and his look of love for me, Donovan, and Joshua. Glen's eyes reflect the tiredness I feel, and I know that he understands, as much as anyone can, how stressful life can be at times. This is also precious to me—the incredibly good relationship that my husband and I have, despite the deep load of homework that he bears and the deep load of "home" work and counselling that I bear.

I see Joshua's sweet smile as he sees me early in the morning and his little arms as they reach for me to envelope me in a huge bear hug. His little voice breathes a sigh of relief as he quietly speaks into my ear, "Mom." He looks at me, smiles, and hugs me again, once more saying his one and only word "Mom." Joshua's excitement at seeing me always makes me feel warm and happy all over. I see Joshua giggle, as we sit at McDonald's for supper, when Donovan gets ketchup all over himself and makes a funny noise. I see Donovan, Joshua, a good friend, and me as we kill time playing with the toys at Wal-Mart, just for fun. The giggles are priceless, and they bring a few giggles from my lips too.

I see my friend listen with gentle, understanding eyes as I tell her of my day and how tired and sick I feel and the good things of the day for the millionth time. A friend willing to hear what is truly on another's heart is more precious than pure gold. I listen as she tells me of her struggles, and I am blessed that she trusts me enough to tell me what is also on her heart. We share a laugh at our "woes" and mutually encourage each other to keep going. This is precious.

I am reminded of Mary, the mother of Jesus, as I write. I would not ever claim to be like Mary. She seems to me to be an incredible kind of woman. She was chosen to be the mother of Jesus, the Son of God! What an incredible privilege! Yet she was an unmarried virgin. Pregnant. The epitome of shame in those days was to be a pregnant, unmarried woman. Who would believe that she saw an angel and was going to bear the Son of God? It never says whom she told, except Joseph. Joseph must have been an incredible man too. He did not want to shame Mary. Quietly, he was going to break their engagement. He must have been very confused about what was going on. Hadn't he chosen a pure woman? Mary had seemed so down to earth, so nice. Yet she was insisting that she had immaculately conceived to bear the Son of God. Now she just seemed plain crazy. Yet Joseph never said any of these thoughts. And God knew better, as He always does. God told Joseph the truth in a dream. Joseph, to his credit, obeyed the words of God and married his betrothed and beloved Mary.

Then when Mary was already pregnant, she made a very long trek out to see her cousin Elizabeth. In modern times, this would have been easy. However, back in Mary's time, it was no easy journey. She probably had to walk for a couple of days to get to Elizabeth's home. When I think back to how sick I was during my pregnancies, I wonder how Mary did it! Perhaps she had a very good pregnancy with no morning sickness (or all-day sickness). Maybe she wasn't so tired and hungry, but what if she was? There is no record of a complaint about her woes when she got to Elizabeth's. The account is life-giving to those who read it. Luke 1:41–56 reads, *"When Elizabeth heard Mary's greeting, the baby leaped in her womb, and Elizabeth was filled with the Holy Spirit. In a loud voice she exclaimed: "Blessed are you among women, and blessed is the child you will bear! But why am I so favored, that the mother of my Lord should come to me? As soon as the sound of your greeting reached my ears, the baby in my womb leaped for joy. Blessed is she who has believed that what the Lord has said to her will be accomplished!"*

And Mary said: "My soul glorifies the Lord and my spirit rejoices in God my Savior, for he has been mindful of the humble state of his servant. From now on all generations will call me blessed, for the Mighty One has done great things for me–holy is his name. His mercy extends to those who fear him, from generation to generation. He has performed mighty deeds with his arm; he has scattered those who are proud in their inmost thoughts. He has brought down rulers from their thrones but has lifted up the humble. He has filled the hungry with good things but has sent the rich away empty. He has helped his servant Israel, remembering to be merciful to Abraham and his descendants forever, even as he said to our fathers."

Mary stayed with Elizabeth for about three months and then returned home."

Now that is humbleness of heart unfolded. Mary and Elizabeth must have been precious friends who filled each other with joy as they both grew closer to God during their miraculous pregnancies.

Then I see Mary, 9-plus months pregnant, riding on a donkey to Bethlehem, just to be counted. *On a donkey! Pregnant!* Wow. Although Biblical scholars differ on the exact night that Jesus was born, it must have been a very tiring and bumpy ride. What amazes me is that regardless of how long Mary and Joseph were in Bethlehem, Jesus was born during their stay there. Look at where she had to give birth. Not in a hospital with midwives, doctors, and nurses standing by to catch the new baby with the latest technology if something went wrong. Mary had to go through labor and give birth to her first-born son in a stable. At that time, a "stable" probably meant a cave that was full of dung from the use of countless sheep and shepherds. A dark place that certainly was not fit for a king. Animals all around.

Darkness, besides the little bit of candlelight. Straw for her bed. Yet she did not complain. We aren't told what kind of labor she had or how long she labored before Jesus was born. The focus is on something much more important. The Son of God was being born that night. It did not matter where He was being born. It did not matter that His mother was probably exhausted and sore from long days of travel on a donkey. It did not matter that complete strangers came as visitors in the dead of night. The focus was on Jesus. Mary's focus was also on Jesus. None of the above mattered to her. She was able to see the bigger picture, not the minute details of what was happening. I'm sure she knew all the details and tried to figure it out, yet her focus was on the miracle. Her focus was on God and his words to her. Her focus was on Jesus and the blessing of being chosen to be His mother. Luke 2:19 says, *"But Mary treasured up all these things and pondered them in her heart."*

What an incredible example to all mothers. Children are a blessing from God. What a divine privilege it is to raise children. The time for them to grow is short. I choose to keep looking for the blessings. I have been chosen to bear Donovan and Joshua. Each of them has a perfect plan from God, if they choose to obey it. I am blessed to raise them in the knowledge and goodness of Jesus Christ. Though some days are trying and I am dead tired, I choose to be like Mary. I will look for each and every minute blessing. I will focus on the bigger picture of Jesus Christ and His daily message to me. I will treasure up each and every blessing. I will ponder these blessings in my heart, holding them dear for years to come.

Chapter Ten

"Daddy"

Recently, my husband was doing a paper on "Attachment Theory" for his Master's degree in counselling. The basic theory is that babies need to bond with their primary caregiver. Whether this person is a healthy, functional person, or an unhealthy, dysfunctional person, will determine whether the child will have attachment problems in the future. For his paper, Glen was trying to find support for the positive influence of fathers and found very little statistical research on the topic. Personally, I believe that dads are intrinsic to the young lives that they have helped bring into the world. There is a definite reason why it takes two to make a baby!

When Glen is around and plays with Donovan and Joshua, it makes a huge difference in their little lives. Every morning, both boys ask the same question, "Where's Daddy?" Donovan, being the older of the two, is starting to understand that Daddy has gone to work, and he asks the question less. Joshua has started "working" in his play. With a twinkle in his eye and a smile on his adorable face, he flies in on his little car to wherever I happen to be and announces, "I'm working, Mommy." His "working" is play, but he is learning something here—a strong work ethic that my husband learned from his father, and he is passing it on to our sons. It is Daddy's responsibility to go to work; that is his role in our family. When Glen comes home, they love to play with him and "help" him in home repair and maintenance.

They also learn that daddies are not home as much as mommies. This is something that is different in every home—some mothers work more than some fathers. In our home, I jam a 20-hour work week into two long working days. This way I can be home more for the boys, and they spend less time with the baby-sitter. We are also very fortunate to have my parents to baby-sit and care for them, which in our case is a huge blessing. I would also hasten to add that I am privileged to be raising children with my husband and not as a single parent. I cannot imagine how difficult it would be to have the huge task of parenting with only one person, as either a single mother or father. Because I work less than Glen, our sons are seeing me as the primary caregiver and miss *me* even more when *I* go to work. Their attachment is bonded primarily to me. However, their attachment to Dad is still very strong. It has been absolutely thrilling to watch Donovan move from complete dependence on me to wanting to go for a ride with Dad to the hardware store. In some ways, it's sad because I am no longer the center of Donovan's world. Yet much more of me is happy to see the independence and healthy self-image that is being formed through both parents. Donovan and Joshua are blessed to have both of us here so that they can have healthy role models to follow. They see Glen working, and they want to do that. They see me working inside the home, working outside the home, and playing with them as much as possible and learn that Mom is not always going to be there. This, according to psychological theories, is a good thing for them because it helps them gain independence. Healthy self-image is given to them in the many hours of play and encouragement that both Glen and I try to give them.

Donovan and Joshua are also blessed by having a Dad that wants to spend time with his family. The other day we were out on a short hike. Donovan started out holding Dad's hand, then moved to me, then back and forth throughout the whole hike, depending on which one of us was more involved with Joshua. It was really neat to see how he felt completely comfortable with both of us and good to see how he didn't want to hurt our feelings by leaving either one of us out. I want to make sure that we affirm him in this act of fair play with others, while reassuring him that we both love him very much, no matter how much time he gets with either of us. Time is also a gift that I strive to give my children. Time is something that can never be taken away—a precious gift. Daddy's presence and the time that he invests make things in the household run much more smoothly. Somehow, his presence is calming, fun, and stable all at the same time. Glen's presence gives the boys a much-needed sense of stability. Because Glen and I are completely committed to each other, no matter what, it gives Donovan and Joshua security, love, and stability in their lives. The life of a toddler and preschooler is tumultuous and full of rolling emotions. They are testing boundaries, learning values, ethics, and morals, much like that of a teenager but at a different level. If both Mom and Dad can be there as a constant stability during their lives, an amazing thing happens in the life of a child. They are given acceptance, love, and belonging, which leads to a healthy self-image that is based on reality, which in turn leads to their acceptance, love, and belonging of others, which carries on a beautifully healthy, cyclical pattern throughout the generations and within their friendships.

Again, I am reminded of Mary and Joseph. We know more about Mary because she was with Jesus in more stories. The assumption, especially because Jesus asked his beloved disciple John to take care of his mother while he hung on the cross, is that Joseph had died at some earlier point. We don't know a lot about their parenting skills, but we do know a little bit. For instance, we know that Joseph was a good man who went against his religious laws and wed Mary anyway, even though she was pregnant out of wedlock. That gave ground for divorce (or calling off the wedding) or even Mary's death. Joseph followed what God said, not what man said, which says much about his stature, integrity, and strength of character. This enabled Jesus to be born into a two-parent family, which is God's design to begin with and for good reason. Parenting together means the burdens and the joys can be shared, which passes on a healthy self-image to children.

We also know that Joseph and Mary were both very worried when they could not find the 12-year-old Jesus as they returned home from the temple at Jerusalem in Luke 2:41–50. What parent wouldn't have been worried? They both went back to Jerusalem to find Jesus together. It is not recorded what they did with their other children at that point. Perhaps the other kids carried on the journey home with relatives or friends. Perhaps the other kids went with Mary and Joseph back to Jerusalem in search of Jesus. What we do know is that both Mary and Joseph went together to search for Jesus.

This is an important part of the story that is overlooked. In every passage of Scripture that we are given about Mary and Joseph they are acting together, in love for one another and in love for those they are ministering to. Whether it was Jesus' birth or going to the temple to dedicate Jesus or escaping Caesar Augustus, we are given a picture of Mary and Joseph together. Of course, we are not given any play-by-play, word by word conversation between the two, but I like to imagine that a man so full of integrity as Joseph, this man who was chosen to be the human father of Christ, was deeply in love with Mary and an incredible parent.

Incredible parenting happens as a team effort. There are many times when Glen and I resemble tag team wrestlers— minus the wrestling part—as we parent our boys. Getting them to bed on time, as a prime example, always goes better with both of us present. I bathe them, change them, and start reading them stories while Glen tidies up the house a bit and makes their nighttime snack of a vitamin drink. Then we each grab a boy and brush his teeth, make sure he goes "potty" one more time before bed, and pray together as a family. This is a precious time together, but it can feel very stressful if one or both are having trouble with the desire to go to bed! Done as a team, it is one of my most precious times of the day. I get to hold both boys on my lap, read them stories, and for however long they sit, I can hug them. I love it! It is made more possible in my life because Glen carries some of the load, a fact that is certainly not lost on Donovan and Joshua. They know beyond any doubt that Daddy loves them just as much as Mommy does.

While just one person can be an incredible parent, as many are forced to do in this world, Mary and Joseph give us a good example of "team" parenting. They are in it together, for better or for worse. This is the example that Glen and I strive to follow. If God entrusted His only Son to Mary and Joseph to raise, then obviously He knew what He was doing and what would be best for Jesus. Together, parenting can become a double blessing. Children need a Mom, and children need a Dad. I thank God for my husband and that I am not raising Donovan and Joshua without their father, as some are forced to do. I thank God for the beautiful example of team parenting given to us through Mary and Joseph. May God's blessing be upon all parents, as together they form attachments—permanent, healthy bonds with their kids.

Chapter Eleven
My Amazing Friend

I have an amazing friend. She's an absolute miracle worker in my opinion. She drops by during the times when I need her most. In fact, I'm almost sure she is an angel sent by God, specifically for me.

The other day my friend Sandy dropped by to find me in the midst of not one, but two crying boys—not an unusual sight at our home these days, but still a tough situation. Did you know that children don't cry alone? I think they have their own secret language that says when one is upset the other must be too. That way they can really confuse Mom, and she won't know which one to go to first. Maybe they think that the first to be calmed is the one most loved or something. I hope not because that is definitely not how it works! I love them both, even when they are both crying and driving me up a wall.

When my friend, Sandy, walked in, my two sweeties were crying—loudly. She sized up the situation with a quick, gentle glance, looked at me with the most empathetic look ever extended, and said, "Come on, Donovan. Let's go play hockey." Then she took a very excited 2-year-old downstairs, which allowed me to nurse Joshua—the original problem. Bless Sandy's heart. Donovan adores her. She adores him. She's even learning how to hold a baby and change diapers since knowing me.

Yet her angelic abilities did not stop there. My amazing

friend let me shower, a real time dilemma for moms with young children. When do you take a shower when you do not even have time to sit down and can't leave two young children unattended? Then she stayed for supper and did the dreaded counter full of dirty dishes while I nursed Joshua again and changed diapers again. Glorious day! A clean kitchen! Fed and full boys. A fed and full Mommy. A real adult person to talk to—another precious gift with Glen trucking so much and going to school. Then to top it off, she walked with us to the park and back, chasing after Donovan—which is no small task—so that I didn't ever have to leave Joshua alone, even for a second. When we came home, a happy and tired Donovan went promptly to bed. Joshua soon fell asleep to the lull of our voices. Sandy, whose visit was unplanned to begin with, bid me farewell. I rushed to bed and awaited my husband's arrival back from a long trucking shift, while I received the sweet gift of slumber—more relaxed than I otherwise might have been.

I think that God gives us angels when we are desperately in need. God seems to know our ups and downs. He knows when I am so tired that I just cannot possibly take another minute of crying. He knows just how much we can take and when we need an angel to come alongside and help us bear the burden. *Galatians 6:2–4 says, "Bear one another's burdens, and so fulfill the law of Christ. For if anyone thinks himself to be something, when he is nothing, he deceives himself. But let each one examine his own work, and then he will have rejoicing in himself alone, and not in another. For each one shall bear his own load."*

We are not to compare ourselves to others, nor think that we are more than we are—negatively or positively. Our power, our sense of worth, our identity, is all based on one power source as a Christian. This power source is God and God alone. If Jesus Christ lives within us, we are then able to carry our own load as Galatians 6:4 suggests, because a load is what we are reasonably able to carry. However, a burden is more than one person can carry. God made others so that we don't have to go alone.

We are the body of Christ, and He wants us, even instructs us, to help each other with our burdens. We cannot take another's load because that is theirs. We *can* help bear each other's burdens. This is made possible by the abundant power of Jesus Christ, because we can be a unique vessel that Jesus works through and empowers. We can help be the burden bearers, and then we can pass that burden on to Jesus instantly so that *we* are not unnecessarily burdened. What a beautiful picture!

It reminds me of Mary, the mother of Jesus. When she became pregnant with Jesus, she went to visit her amazing friend and cousin, Elizabeth, who was also pregnant with her first child. Perhaps Elizabeth was a burden-bearing friend to Mary. They both had many concerns to ponder and share with each other. Perhaps in the three months that they spent together, they both bore each others' burdens. Most certainly, they talked about the wonder and amazement of both of their pregnancies. They were there for each other during a time of need, wonder, and amazement. We do not know the details of their discussions. We don't know what they treasured in their hearts during that precious time of being pregnant with their first miracle children, Jesus the Son of God and John the Baptist.

The baby that was born to Mary, virgin mother, is also there for us at all times. He's not an angel, which the Bible says cannot be exalted any more than mere humans. Jesus is our immortal Savior, the Son of God. He came to earth to save us from our sins and be the bridge between God and us. Jesus is our intercessor who stands before God and shows us to God as He sees us, washed white as snow with His shed blood from the cross. Jesus wants to live in the most unlikely of places—our hearts. This is something like the manger or feed trough that He was placed in upon birth. Our hearts aren't clean, but His presence can wash us as white as snow. His presence in an *unclean* environment, such as a feed trough, made it clean. We are the temple of a living and Almighty God. With all this in mind, how can we not know that Jesus is going to send us physical angels every once in a while, especially when we are really in need and cannot take anymore? Jesus' angels serve Him and us through their acts of kindness and goodness. Angels in our day and age are just as real as angels in Mary's time. I thank God for the precious angels like Sandy in my life. I thank God for making me His holy dwelling place. May I be filled with His grace and love so that I can also be a burden bearer for others, including my precious boys.

Chapter 12

Angels Watching Over

When Joshua learned to walk at eleven and a half months, things in our household went from crazy to chaotic. He was into absolutely everything—every kitchen drawer was emptied neatly and stacked up around the kitchen and dining room. Every clothes drawer left open would soon be emptied, strewn across the room in babyhood rebellion and glee. The bathroom door could never be left open, period. One day I found three pairs of shoes and a large towel stuffed neatly into the toilet bowl. This was not exactly what I had hoped to find then or any day.

Keeping in mind that Joshua could move very fast, I always tried to cover my bases wherever I went. One day I walked into my chiropractor's office, which is located on the corner of two busy streets. As the day was not particularly warm, I asked the receptionist if she minded my closing the front door, explaining that Joshua would run out if it was left open. She consented so I closed the door and was soon led into the chiropractor's patient room with Donovan and Joshua in tow. I didn't bother closing the patient room door, reasoning that I had already closed the main door and explained my reasoning to the receptionist. My boys would be all right, even if they wandered into the main waiting room area where the toys were located. With this in mind, I was not concerned as I lay on the chiropractic table and heard Donovan say, "Mommy, Joshua walked out the door!"

"Oh, he should be okay, Donovan. Mommy closed the front door so he can't go outside," I replied.

Not more than one minute later, I heard a strange woman's voice asking, "Is this someone's baby?"

The myriad of thoughts that go through one's mind at a moment like that is incomprehensible. I jumped off the table, one step behind the chiropractor. I heard something about a baby standing on the yellow line, grabbed my Joshua, who was then being held by the chiropractor, and walked back into the patient room, not seeing more than the back of the woman's head who had saved my baby.

Looking back, I know that I was in severe shock. I got the boys in the car after the receptionist apologized profusely for opening the front door. As I climbed into the driver's seat, the tears started to come. I shook like a leaf for at least the next two hours. I had almost lost my baby. So many things could have happened to him that day. He could have been hit by a car. He could have been kidnapped. He could have just wandered away and got lost. But God sent an angel to shelter and protect my boy so that he didn't even experience any trauma. As I drove home, I realized that I didn't know who the woman was that saved Joshua. I didn't ask her how she knew to come into that office. I didn't know where she found him. I didn't thank her for the most incredible thing a stranger can do—save a life. I will wonder for the rest of my life who this angel was that came into my life quickly and vanished even faster. Was she a real person that God placed there that day? Was she an angel? Or was it angels that surrounded Joshua and kept him from physical and emotional harm, while other angels led this wonderful woman to bring my Joshua back to me? And why didn't I have the presence of mind to thank her? These are things I will never know this side of heaven. What I do know is that I am incredibly grateful to this stranger, Joshua's angel, for saving him.

Many things have happened to my Joshua since then. I am convinced that children have angels watching over them because Joshua is proof of that fact. A few months ago, I caught him by the ankle as he dove head first out of his high chair, about to land on the ceramic tile floor. How my reflexes worked so fast at that moment is beyond my comprehension; however, I am convinced that God had a lot to do with it.

Today was another example of God protecting my Joshua. As I turned to pull the blind in Donovan's room for night, I heard a cry behind me, turned, and grabbed a heavy bureau full of clothes with paraphernalia set on top of it as it came crashing down on top of Joshua. Somehow, my hand, which was given super strength, and a small stool managed to catch the bureau. After catching the bureau, I still didn't know if Joshua was crushed or not. I couldn't get the bureau to stand, because it was now wobbly from its fall, and my strength was waning. As if in some sort of surreal nightmare that plays in slow motion, I heard myself scream, "Sandy, help!" (My friend had only moments before dropped by to chat and was waiting in the kitchen for me while I put the boys to bed.) Sandy came running and held up the bureau while I held a screaming Josh, wondering if every bone in his body was broken. He came out completely unscathed, except for his fingers that got a bit bruised. Besides scaring Sandy, Donovan, himself, and me half to death, we all were fine.

Again, I realized that God is watching over my boys and me. He has appointed a time for all to go back to Him. My boys are just here as a gift from God, and I know not how long this gift will last. My heart cries for those who have lost children. I cannot imagine the agony that they must go through; the loss that pierces their hearts. I cannot even imagine receiving comfort from the same God that I had asked a thousand different times to tell me "Why?" Yet I do know that God does give comfort to those who mourn. He has a reason and a time for everything, and our minds are not big enough to understand the thousands of why's and how comes. Someday, all will be known, and we will see the bigger picture. For now, all we have is a piece of the puzzle. Sometimes that piece hurts. Sometimes it brings comfort. Sometimes we get the whole puzzle here on earth, and other times we are told to be content with our current knowledge. Yet we need to rely on a faith that is bigger than the pain and the questions that sometimes come. It is a faith that fully believes that God knows what He is doing and that He loves us unconditionally. It is a faith that fully believes that God does all things for good, and that He would never harm His children.

This always reminds me of Mary, the mother of Jesus. When the angel, Gabriel, came to tell her that she had found favor with God and was chosen to bear His child in the flesh, she must have had questions. She asked only one . . ."How can this be?" She was a virgin, betrothed to be married. If she by some miracle became pregnant the chances of her fiancée having her put to death as the Jewish law allowed would be great. Gabriel explained the miracle of what was about to happen. God's spirit would come to her and she would conceive, bearing the child whom she was to name Jesus. He would be the King of kings and Lord of lords. Mary simply listened, heard God's command, and obeyed willingly and with great joy.

Mary must have known the hardships that she would go through as the mother of the Son of God. She must have known the prophesies about Jesus dying. Yet she accepted the assignment with joy. She stood at the foot of His cross and watched Him die an agonizing death. She listened as her next assignment came, and Jesus entrusted her to the care of His beloved disciple, John, as his adopted mother. Mary lost Jesus one day, then got Him back three days later when He rose from the dead. She physically lost Him again when He ascended into Heaven to be with his Father. The emotions running through her body during those days must have been inconceivable. Knowing some of the prophesies about Jesus probably didn't prepare her for watching Him die. Yet she was a woman of godly character and strength. Blessings untold must have followed Mary for her obedience and faith. She knew that Jesus could perform miracles, because she asked Jesus to help at the wedding where he turned the water into wine. How many miracles must she have witnessed during Jesus' precious growing up years?

Mary bore great humility and graciously gave back to God the gift that He had bestowed upon her, the incredible responsibility of raising his only child. No matter what length of time God chooses to bestow the gifts of Donovan and Joshua on me, I gladly and joyously accept these gifts as from God. May God continue to guide me with his wisdom. May God continue to grace my household with angels, watching over us as a shield from harm . . . until the day God calls us each home.

Epilogue

Today was Donovan's first day of grade two, and Joshua's meet-the- kindergarten-teacher day. Strange, exciting, and sad feelings run through me as I see my two little boys taking steps into the big world where I cannot always be there for them. On one hand, I am excited about these two new creatures, whom I call my sons and whom I love dearly, becoming incredible people with amazing, fun, and witty personalities. I am excited about them growing up and the friendships and bonds that I have already formed with them. I am excited about years to come and meeting their future spouses, and my future grand children, all of whom I am already praying for. Yet there is also a feeling of fear as I leave them in their classrooms and walk out, not ever really finding out what happens in every moment of their days. What if they are left out? What if the other children don't want to play with them? What if a stranger takes them? The "what-ifs" could easily turn into large scale fears and paranoia's of the most horrible scenarios that could happen to two wonderful little boys.

In those "what-if" moments, I am reminded of whose children Donovan and Joshua really are. God gently whispers into my fears of His love for me, and His love for my boys. I John 4:18 says, *"There is no fear in love. But perfect love drives out fear, because fear has to do with punishment. The one who fears is not made perfect in love."*

Knowing that Jesus loved me enough to die for me and rise again allows me to hold onto the promises of God. God always fulfills His promises for us, His children. He made us. He made me. He made my sons and entrusted them to me for awhile to raise and care for and love. Yet God has not deserted us during this time of growing up. Yes, bad things happen to good people. Yet within all the bad and evil in the world, God is there protecting His children. God never promised us that life would be perfect here on earth. God, in fact, promised us exactly the opposite. 1 Peter 4:12 and 13 states, *"Dear friends, do not be surprised at the painful trial you are suffering, as though something strange were happening to you. But rejoice that you participate in the suffering of Christ, so that you may be overjoyed when his glory is revealed."*

We will experience pain and trials here in this world. Donovan and Joshua already experience pain and trials here in this world. Joshua is nervous about kindergarten. Donovan has to face this year in school without his best friend from birth being there with him. Already today he said that no one chose him to play on a foot ball team at recess. He felt too left out to say anything. Everything in me wants to run in there and rescue my children. Yet rescuing them would not help them learn to be assertive and make new friends. It is in the pain that happens in this world, and the trials that we face that the Master Potter is molding us into His character. He is perfecting us and helping us to run this great race until the day we arrive at our true home in the Heavenly realm and Jesus meets us with a big smile on His beautiful face, His arms extended wide, and His booming yet gentle voice welcoming us home.

It is my goal to be a good role model running the race for Jesus. My aim is to please and glorify Christ Jesus in all that I do, including being a Mom. Part of glorifying Jesus is to trust Him not only with my life, but also with the lives of my sons. When I begin to fear for them, Jesus fills me with His incredible love that drives out fear. When I begin to fear, Jesus reminds me that Donovan and Joshua are His beloved sons. When I tell Jesus that I am scared for my boys because I cannot always save them and be there for them, He gently reminds me that He can and always will be with them. When the boys are in trouble and need extra prayer, Jesus also gently brings them to my mind and tells me how to pray for them. This is what my Jesus does for me, for Donovan and Joshua. He loves us, He cares for us, and He walks with us every step of the way.

Although it seems that the world is full of chaos, in reality God is in control. I can trust God to help me raise my children, and also to take care of my children when I cannot be there for them. I choose to allow God to be my pilot. I choose to give God control and to trust Him with every minute detail of my life. God is a God of love and wants good things for His children so I cling to that promise.

May God richly bless you as you journey down your own path of parenthood. I challenge you to choose to trust the loving and caring God who is our Creator to also pilot you in your life's race. I echo Joshua in saying, *"As for me and my house, we will serve the Lord."* (Joshua 24:15)

Bibliography

Barber, Katherine *The Canadian Oxford Dictionary* Oxford University Press Canada, Oxford, Ont. 1998

Brother Lawrence *The Practice of the Presence of God* Whitaker House, United States. 1982

(End Notes)

[1] Barber, Katherine *Oxford Canadian Dictionary* Oxford University Press Canada., Ontario 1998 p. 1545

Contact Laurel Hildebrandt
www.laurelhildebrandt.com

or order more copies of this book at

TATE PUBLISHING, LLC

127 East Trade Center Terrace
Mustang, Oklahoma 73064

(888) 361 - 9473

Tate Publishing, LLC

www.tatepublishing.com